THE SECRET LANGUAGE
OF SLEEP

*A Couple's Guide
to the Thirty-Nine Positions*

Endless thanks to photographer/model Marco Baroz; models Brian Mello,
Heidi Pollock, Scout Shannon, Stephen E. Smith, and Jill Stauffer;
editors Dave Eggers and Eli Horowitz; copyeditor Jordan Bass;
designers Henry Chen and Sasha Wizansky; feedbackers Paul Adams,
Gene Astadan, Jay Patrikios, and Kristin Windbigler;
and parents Ariel, Dan, Frank, and Pat.

THE SECRET LANGUAGE
OF SLEEP

A Couple's Guide to the Thirty-Nine Positions

By Evany Thomas

Illustrated by Amelia Bauer

M^cSWEENEY'S IRREGULARS

SAN FRANCISCO

For more information about McSweeney's, visit www.mcsweeneys.net.

Copyright © 2006 Evany Thomas, Amelia Bauer, and McSweeney's

ISBN: 1-932416-47-1

INTRODUCTION

Should you take the job in Finland? Move in with the radiologist? Buy a horse? Bury the bloodied scrunchie in the dog park? When it comes to the big decisions, the times in our lives when we find ourselves staring down the barrel of potential regret, most of us turn to our friends, our therapists, and mounted policemen for guidance. Yet the one place that holds all the answers—our beds—we tend to ignore completely.

We spend a third of our lives on that 60-by-80 inch* stretch of springs and foam padding. It's the stage where our dramas unfold, the boxing ring where we settle our differences, the garden where love, commitment, and sexy-type feelings take root. A couple's bed is the true

---

* Queen: 60-by-80 inch; King: 76-by-80 inch; Full: 54-by-75 inch; Twin: 39-by-75 inch

resting place of their subconscious, the quiet spot where all their secret motivations, needs, and scents linger. Awake, we may think we know what we're doing, and why. But each night, as we settle into our favorite sleeping position, the truth escapes.

Some couples—Tetherballers or Crime Scenesters, for starters—sleep far apart, yet always with a reassuring hand on their mate's hip. Some sleep wrapped tightly together, their dreams and exhalations intermingled (Melting Spoons or Patient Doctors). Your pose might be somewhere in between: Paper Dolls, perhaps, or the Starfish and Conch. Finding your pose isn't that difficult; there are just thirty-nine potential poses in all, each of which is illustrated in the pages that follow.

Once you locate your default pose, everything else falls into place. Armed with your "bed truth," mysteries from past failed relationships are solved. (Q: Why does no one understand your nighttime weeping? A: Because you are a Downward Koala, looking for the support of the right Tree.) Puzzling or worrisome behaviors, such as a strong need to be weighted down by 140 pounds of love, finally make sense (your Bread just needed Spreading). And the answers to all your life's thorny questions—where to live, who to love, which job to quit—now all seem perfectly clear.

SOME OTHER WAYS TO USE THIS GUIDE

The way you sleep is more than a diagnostic tool; it's also an opportunity for change. In some cases, a couple can reverse-engineer their fate by switching to the sleeping pose that promotes the kind of qualities they crave. Couples in pursuit of a perfect pose are strongly encouraged to keep a sleep diary (a notebook stored close to the bed or a remote-triggered camera mounted on the ceiling). Continue with your experimentation and daily recordings until you find what works. Then just watch as, over the upcoming weeks or even the next few nights, your relationship grows and thrives, your energy improves, and one by one all your goals as a couple are achieved.

Couples who are still in the market for a perfect pose and have no idea where to begin may want to let their "comfort zone" guide them. Each of the thirty-nine positions is sorted into one of four zones: Sun, Sea, Wind, or Wood. The positions found in a particular zone all share certain themes in common, and couples who like the general sound of, say, the Wind Zone, should spend some time exploring each of the nine different Wind poses: the vulnerability of Bird in Hand, the legal troubles of Softserve Swirl, the deep regrets of the Ventriloquist, and so on.

Even couples well familiar with their chosen position can benefit from zone exploration. Periodically, take a week off from a cherished pose; the corresponding feelings of "sleeping with someone new" have been known to lengthen the lifespan of love. And you never know—as time passes and personalities mellow, couples sometimes outgrow their pose. It may be time for you and your mate to go hunting once again for the pose that perfectly reflects your evolved thirsts, needs, or advancing osteoporosis.

LEGEND

A good choice when one or both snore   📢

Can be soothing for digestive ailments   ☕

Proven morning mood elevator   🚡

Can cause unusually intense or vivid dreaming   🐷

Preferred position of people who work on their feet   👢

Promotes sleep in some insomniacs   Z!

Works well in outdoor situations (sleeping bags)   ⛺

Can accommodate third parties (pets, babies, etc.)   👫

May require a larger bed   🛏

Works well in smaller bedding situations   🛏

Suitable for warmer climates   ☀

Suitable for colder climates   ❄

SECTION ONE
the sun sleepers

The one unifying aspect of all Sun pose couples is that they always sleep facing the same side of the bed, their bodies aligned front to back, lined up like Girl Scouts eagerly waiting for a chance to donate blood or apply a cold compress to a burn victim.

This desire to give aid to people in need runs throughout all the Sun poses, which attract helpful, warm, and startlingly enthusiastic couples. In some cases (The Heimlich, Spoons, and The Seatbelt), Sun posers bring a sense of ready safety nets and airbags poised for rescue to the bed. Other poses, such as the Big C Little c and Tandem Cycle, demonstrate the Sun Sleeper's affection for the great outdoors and almost any sport that risks bodily injury. And like the badges, patches, and sashes that motivate actual campfire girls, Sun posers' goals—perfectly toned abdominals, a multimillion-dollar 401k, or a "tickle machine" factory—can be all-encompassing (as typified by Tobogganers).

Bonus: a small subset of Sun couples gravitates to the side-focused nature of the positions purely out of a shared desire to watch television while still holding on to each other.

CLASSIC SPOONS

Simple, romantic, tried, and true, Spoons (or Spooning) is easily the most well known of the Sun positions. Cynics attribute its popularity to the position's mind-numbing simplicity, but those who dismiss Classic Spoons as too easy, or overly quaint, simply are not doing it right.

On the surface, the pose is deceptively simple: couples lie on their sides, stomach pressed against back. Less tangible and far more difficult to master is the shared feeling of warmth and contentment that comes from a successful Spooning. Done correctly, a true Spoon can elevate a couple's collective temperature to over 100 degrees and cause their mouths to fill with an unexplained sweetness. This level of Spooning is rare—only one couple in a hundred can achieve it—and it has absolutely nothing to do with practice. A couple exploring their first night together is as capable of performing champion-caliber Spoons as a couple celebrating their ivory anniversary.

Unlike the more strictly defined positions (Fireman's Carry, Venn Trick, etc.), leg and arm placement in Classic Spoons is wide open to interpretation. As a result, Spoon configurations vary tremendously from region to region or even house to house. A couple could spend an entire lifetime exploring all of Spoons' possibilities, and indeed many do.

CLASSIC SPOONS

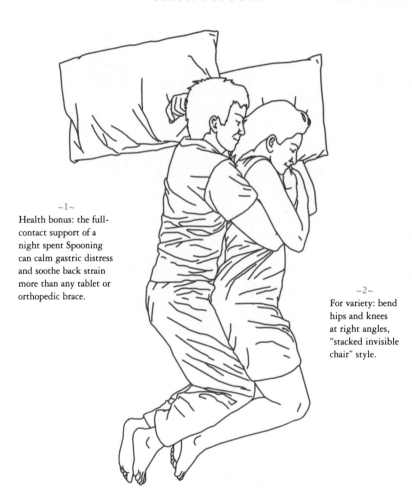

~1~
Health bonus: the full-contact support of a night spent Spooning can calm gastric distress and soothe back strain more than any tablet or orthopedic brace.

~2~
For variety: bend hips and knees at right angles, "stacked invisible chair" style.

MELTING SPOONS

The Melting Spoons position is very closely related to the Classic, the main difference being the placement of the couple's arms and feet. Just as the pose itself lacks firm internal boundaries, Melting Spoons couples typically suffer from an almost crippling interdependence. They have great trouble making decisions on their own, and will call their mates from department store dressing rooms for detailed purchasing advice. Is this item worth the cost? Where, and with what, will it be worn? Is it machine washable or dry clean only? Meanwhile, at work, Melting Spooners are often mistaken for diligent employees, thanks to all their feverish emailing and instant messaging.

Many Melting Spooners, particularly those raised by hyper-controlling parents, have no problem with this unwholesome setup. But couples who find they actually miss the luxury of independent thought are advised to limit themselves to the Classic for as many nights as it takes to regain a sense of self.

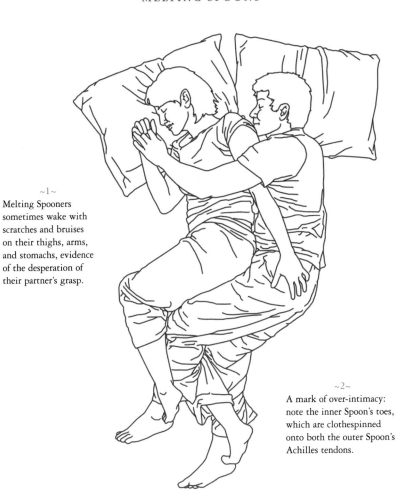

~1~
Melting Spooners
sometimes wake with
scratches and bruises
on their thighs, arms,
and stomachs, evidence
of the desperation of
their partner's grasp.

~2~
A mark of over-intimacy:
note the inner Spoon's toes,
which are clothespinned
onto both the outer Spoon's
Achilles tendons.

TOBOGGAN

Alpine experience can be helpful but is not at all necessary. To achieve a Toboggan in your own home, the Mountain (FIGURE B) should settle into the bed alone, lying on one side. After pausing to allow the Mountain's breath to settle and regulate (five minutes), the Toboggan (FIGURE A) steps onto the bed and, in one fluid motion, 1) crouches deeply, 2) falls forward, and 3) rolls to the side, landing with feet and back tucked snuggly against the Mountain.

What makes couples who choose the Toboggan unique? The intensity of their drive. They always, without question, arrive at any goal or destination well ahead of their group of friends. They're the first to open a retirement savings account, the first to replace their futon with a mattress of consequence, the first to resort to loose-fitting, elastic-waisted, crinkle-cottoned clothing.

Tobogganing couples must be careful to make sure, in their headlong rush to early-adopt, that their goals are properly defined and truly shared. Otherwise they risk racing off in two completely different directions, and suddenly one morning the Mountain wakes to 300-thread-count Egyptian cotton sheets and a sparkling downtown loft while the Toboggan greets the sunrise in a truck stop bathroom.

TOBOGGAN

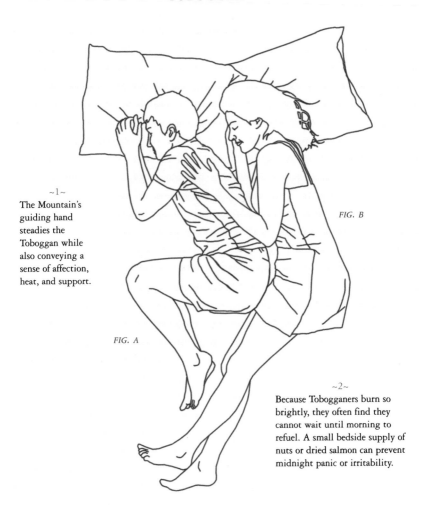

~1~
The Mountain's guiding hand steadies the Toboggan while also conveying a sense of affection, heat, and support.

FIG. B

FIG. A

~2~
Because Tobogganers burn so brightly, they often find they cannot wait until morning to refuel. A small bedside supply of nuts or dried salmon can prevent midnight panic or irritability.

BIG C LITTLE c

Typical of a Sun pose, the Big C Little c position features both parties lying on their sides, back nested against front. What distinguishes this pose from the softer Sun poses is its "anywhere, anytime" attitude, which is what makes this the preferred pose of couples who enjoy spending their free time in the great outdoors.

The simple grace of the "Cc" shape is readily accessible, even to couples separated in two individual sleeping bags. The sturdiness of the pose prevents rolling, which can be a factor for couples sleeping in tents pitched on a grade. And because it's so well suited for camping, in fact synonymous with tent-living for many couples, Big C Little c can bring a welcome sense of wilderness adventure into the comfort, safety, and softness of your own bed.

To enhance the sensation of the outdoors brought indoors, try smoking your pillowcases over a wood-burning grill to capture the essence of a campfire. A handful of sand sprinkled between the sheets and a once-per-week showering schedule recreates the rugged grittiness of "roughing it," while a "Sounds of the Forest" CD playing softly on the bedside stereo provides the finishing touch.

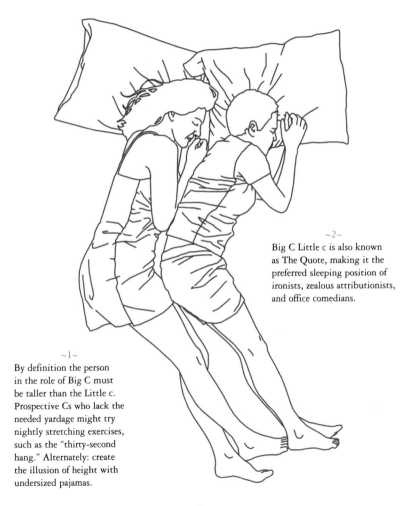

~2~

Big C Little c is also known as The Quote, making it the preferred sleeping position of ironists, zealous attributionists, and office comedians.

~1~

By definition the person in the role of Big C must be taller than the Little c. Prospective Cs who lack the needed yardage might try nightly stretching exercises, such as the "thirty-second hang." Alternately: create the illusion of height with undersized pajamas.

RUNNING MAN

The Running Man is most popular with children of divorced parents, who tend to enter relationships weighed down by all sorts of ideas about what kind of behavior doesn't work (shouting, discretely pouring dishwashing liquid over a mate's salad) and what does (calm, cool, rational silence).

Unfortunately, as anyone with parent rebellion issues soon discovers, the opposite of what you hate isn't always loveable. And the typical Running Man couple's fierce desire to escape the legacy of their parents' embattled lifestyles can sometimes chase away the passion and electricity that comes from healthy disagreement. Over time, their shared silence cools from "companionable" to just "polite."

To defibrillate a flat-lined Running Man relationship, try inviting a measured amount of stress into the mix: hire inexperienced contractors for an expensive remodel, or voluntarily attend comedy traffic school. If that doesn't do it, more visceral scare tactics may be in order: blowing an air horn in the dark of night, removing the bottom step from the staircase, public pantsing, etcetera.

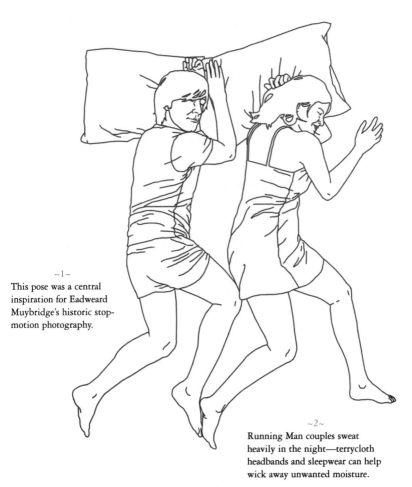

~1~
This pose was a central
inspiration for Eadweard
Muybridge's historic stop-
motion photography.

~2~
Running Man couples sweat
heavily in the night—terrycloth
headbands and sleepwear can help
wick away unwanted moisture.

TANDEM CYCLE

Tandem Cyclists are the stars of the sleeping world. Tan, relaxed, and windswept, they're always smiling bright, no matter what blows life deals. Disease, public speaking, automotive failure—they take it all in stride, thanks (it is believed) to the steadying power of spending night after night with a best-loved mate at their backs.

The flipside of this steadiness is that Tandem Cyclists sometimes get overly confident and court risk unnecessarily. In moderation, meat-eating contests and biathlons provide Tandem Cycle sleepers with a reasonable thrill. But when they take extreme sports to the extreme, Tandem Cyclists put more than their bodies in danger: their relationships are also at risk. Racing shopping carts down at Tetanus Curve may sound alluring, but Tandem Cyclists do well to remember that nothing dampens a partner's sexual heat like having to swab a mate's infected puncture wounds.

As long as Tandem Cycle couples wear their helmets, carry their bear whistles, and make a reasonable effort to avoid injuries, their unique traits—steady confidence and love of danger—make for a potent mix.

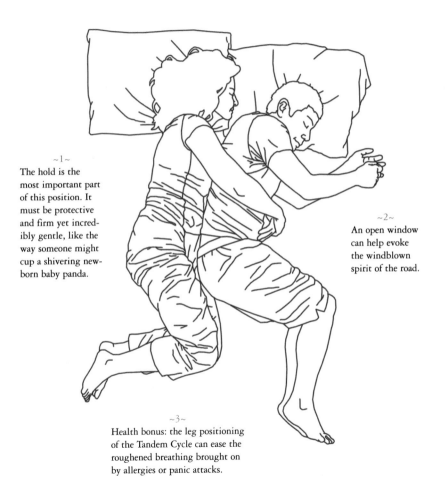

~1~

The hold is the most important part of this position. It must be protective and firm yet incredibly gentle, like the way someone might cup a shivering newborn baby panda.

~2~

An open window can help evoke the windblown spirit of the road.

~3~

Health bonus: the leg positioning of the Tandem Cycle can ease the roughened breathing brought on by allergies or panic attacks.

FLYING BOBS

The Flying Bobs is a pose of happenstance, something to be tumbled into rather than arranged with any deliberation. To get into position, stand at the bottom of the bed and fall sideways. Don't concern yourself with the placement of your feet or arms. If you don't force it, you'll find your bodies fall into position on their own. Just clear your thoughts and relax until you are loose enough to give in to the thrilling, dizzying energy of the Flying Bobs.

The central feature of the Flying Bobs pose is the lack of control it demands from its sleepers, making it the perfect choice for couples who toil under the weight of adulthood's responsibilities and expectations. After a day of acting respectable, of standing in lines and of sitting at desks, a full night of Flying Bobs is well in order.

Formerly tense couples wake after a night of Flying Bobs with cheeks flushed and eyes bright, their bodies reinvigorated and their minds clear and ready to take on another crushing day.

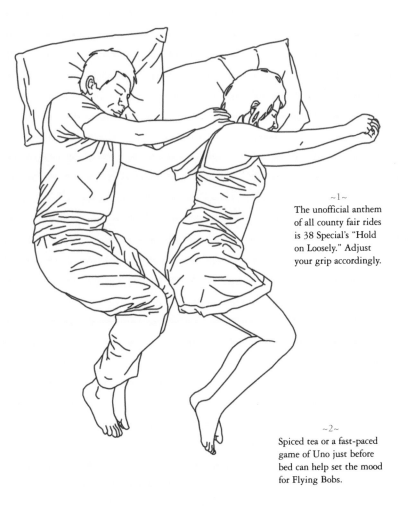

~1~
The unofficial anthem
of all county fair rides
is 38 Special's "Hold
on Loosely." Adjust
your grip accordingly.

~2~
Spiced tea or a fast-paced
game of Uno just before
bed can help set the mood
for Flying Bobs.

THE HEIMLICH

Any first-aid course veteran knows the stance of the life-saving Heimlich maneuver. The namesake sleeping pose features similar positioning: the Rescuer (FIGURE A) grasps the Choker (FIGURE B) from behind, joining both hands into fists just under the Choker's sternum. If this were an actual emergency, the Rescuer would thrust the fists inward rhythmically until whatever blocked the Choker's airway was dislodged. In the case of The Heimlich sleeping pose, no actual stomach pumping is required. Nonetheless, the spirit of a bedmate ready and willing to spring into heroic action infuses the position with a sensation of safety, making it clear that this bed is shared by two people who care very much about each other's well-being.

This impulse to rescue people in need sometimes leaves Heimlich couples vulnerable to con artists or anyone with an overactive sense of entitlement. Unless they take very special care to establish and then vigilantly guard their boundaries, Heimlichers can exhaust themselves supporting unemployable family members, filling in for binging alcoholic coworkers, or helping acquaintances move.

THE HEIMLICH

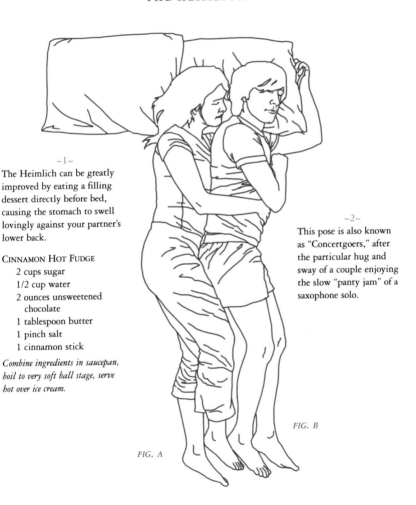

~ 1 ~

The Heimlich can be greatly improved by eating a filling dessert directly before bed, causing the stomach to swell lovingly against your partner's lower back.

CINNAMON HOT FUDGE

- 2 cups sugar
- 1/2 cup water
- 2 ounces unsweetened chocolate
- 1 tablespoon butter
- 1 pinch salt
- 1 cinnamon stick

Combine ingredients in saucepan, boil to very soft ball stage, serve hot over ice cream.

~ 2 ~

This pose is also known as "Concertgoers," after the particular hug and sway of a couple enjoying the slow "panty jam" of a saxophone solo.

FIG. B

FIG. A

THE SEATBELT

Though the protection of an outstretched arm is negligible in the event of an automotive collision, no mother can resist the instinct to try to "catch" her child when surprised with an unexpected stop, even when that child has aged well into adulthood. This kind of long-lasting, knee-jerk love that people feel for a loved one in danger is the foundation upon which The Seatbelt pose is built.

Couples are advised to let their instincts guide them as they settle into the pose. Once the arms of the Seatbelt (FIGURE A) snap into place around the Rider (FIGURE B), the couple can let their fondest memories of motherly love wash over them: the smell of hot laundry, the taste of bland chicken, the relief of loose hairs brushed free from a feverish forehead. (Couples with mothers who fall along nagging or neurotic lines can substitute more generally pleasant thoughts: a deep hot bath, freshly baked bread, cupped elbows, etcetera.)

After steeping in sensations of support and safety, couples awake like baby birds ready for their first flight, the small thrill of "what next" coursing through them.

THE SEATBELT

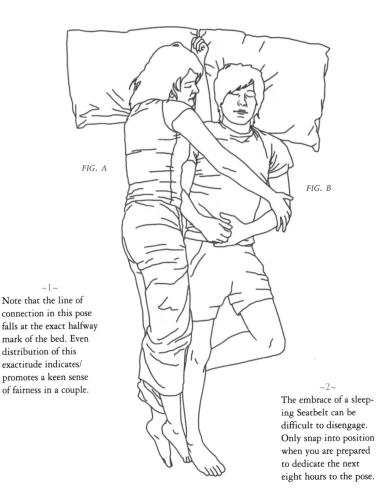

FIG. A

FIG. B

~1~
Note that the line of
connection in this pose
falls at the exact halfway
mark of the bed. Even
distribution of this
exactitude indicates/
promotes a keen sense
of fairness in a couple.

~2~
The embrace of a sleep-
ing Seatbelt can be
difficult to disengage.
Only snap into position
when you are prepared
to dedicate the next
eight hours to the pose.

SECTION TWO
the wind sleepers

The focus of any Wind pose is the way the couple's elements dovetail together. Some Wind pose couples (Zippers or Fireman's Carriers) snap into place bodily, like two pieces of the same puzzle. For other Wind sleepers, the complement comes from meshing temperaments (such as the bickering ebb and tender-apology flow of Starfish and Conch), or a perfect alignment of interlocking desires (the Bread's appetite for a Spread).

There's also an unexpected heroic streak that runs through Wind sleepers. Hunting down a wanted felon (a Softserver favorite) comes with its own risks, but as Fireman's Carry couples know, it can also take courage to agree to a third date after a lifetime running from commitment, or (in the case of Bird in Handers) to try again after long, loving relationships go sour.

BIRD IN HAND

The Bird in Hand is the preferred position of couples who are both on their second marriage (or similarly committed relationship). The experience and wisdom that comes from possessing and then losing love makes Bird in Handers unusually grateful partners, and they revel in the relief of finding themselves in each other's arms night after night.

To prepare for the Bird in Hand pose, stand with legs shoulder-width apart and make a fist with one hand. Grasp your fist with the opposing hand. Lift your elbows high. Feel the strength of the pose; familiarize yourself with its sensuality. Only when you are sure you can recognize this sensation, even in the dark, are you ready to undertake Bird in Hand.

For the first night, concentrate on getting your bodies into correct position. Once you've mastered the physical side of the pose (it can sometimes take two or three nights), you're ready to tackle the emotions. As Hand (FIGURE A), allow the desire to protect take over. Tighten your muscles, round your back into a hardened shield, vocalize your feelings with quieting words... whatever it takes to make your Bird feel safe and warm. As Bird (FIGURE B), allow yourself to feel totally vulnerable—it may be necessary to remove all your clothing or divulge your credit history, but the results will be worthwhile.

🐦 Z! ❄

BIRD IN HAND

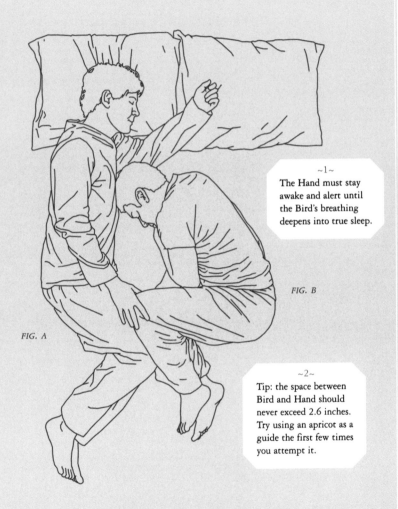

~1~
The Hand must stay
awake and alert until
the Bird's breathing
deepens into true sleep.

FIG. B

FIG. A

~2~
Tip: the space between
Bird and Hand should
never exceed 2.6 inches.
Try using an apricot as a
guide the first few times
you attempt it.

THE VENTRILOQUIST

Over the last twenty years, The Ventriloquist has become the most popular sleeping position in the enviable 21–34 age group. But that wasn't always the case: for centuries the pose was regarded as a gateway to the dark arts, and even prostitution. It wasn't until the late 1970s that the position gained the acceptance and allure it enjoys today.

Spontaneous to the point of mania, Ventriloquist couples like to keep each other guessing by rearranging the furniture, replacing the sugar with salt, or hemming each other's clothing. Ventriloquisters delight in role-playing, and Halloween is their absolute favorite time of year: they find childlike delight in the chance it gives them to go all-out with the costumes, plus all the candy and blood.

Ventriloquist couples also have a tendency to speak without thinking, which sometimes leads to misunderstandings or unemployment. But Ventriloquists' natural charisma is so potent that they easily charm their way into a new job or group of friends.

THE VENTRILOQUIST

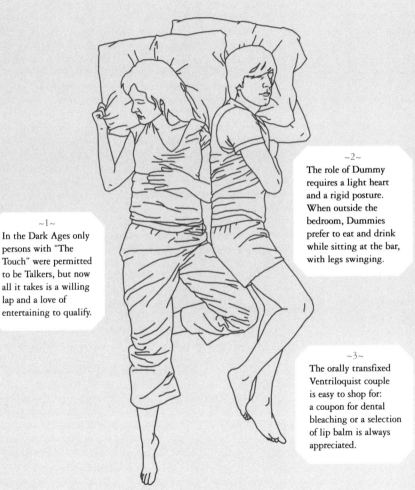

~1~
In the Dark Ages only persons with "The Touch" were permitted to be Talkers, but now all it takes is a willing lap and a love of entertaining to qualify.

~2~
The role of Dummy requires a light heart and a rigid posture. When outside the bedroom, Dummies prefer to eat and drink while sitting at the bar, with legs swinging.

~3~
The orally transfixed Ventriloquist couple is easy to shop for: a coupon for dental bleaching or a selection of lip balm is always appreciated.

EXCALIBUR

The legend of the Sword in the Stone tells us that only the one, true king can remove the sword from its enchanted mooring. Yet sometimes a sword and stone are so good together, even Arthur himself would hesitate to separate them.

Excalibur couples are exactly that kind of match. It isn't that they're more compatible than other people—they battle as much as the next couple. The attraction is purely visual. The combined form of the Excalibur couple is to the eye what a minor chord is to the ear: haunting, chilling, and thrilling. The kind of couple that most typifies this golden mean are the giant, bulging weightlifters who always seem to join forces with gymnast-small mates. Very tall women paired with short men can sometimes do the trick. It's startling how close to wrong that right sits, and the genius of Excalibur unions is that they only barely manage to fall on the good side of the equation.

The first hurdle for aspiring Excaliburs is getting your feet into position. Start with both sleepers lying side by side. The Sword (FIGURE B) turns toward the Stone (FIGURE A). Using the knee of the leg closest to the ceiling, Sword nudges under Stone's left leg. Stone then folds left leg over Sword's top leg. Finally, Stone nestles left foot under Sword's lower knee. Does this feel comfortable to you? Excalibur: excelsior!

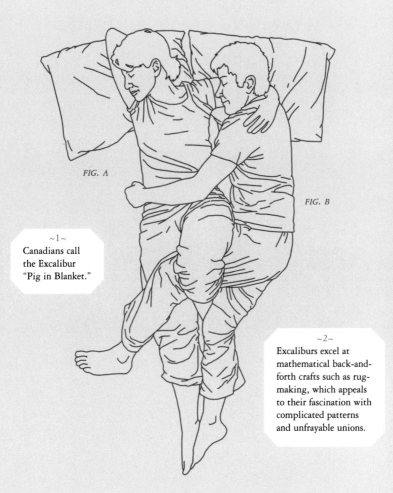

FIG. A

FIG. B

~1~
Canadians call
the Excalibur
"Pig in Blanket."

~2~
Excaliburs excel at
mathematical back-and-
forth crafts such as rug-
making, which appeals
to their fascination with
complicated patterns
and unfrayable unions.

PINCHING KOALA AND TREE

When the Pinching Koala is implemented correctly, the dreams of both Koala (FIGURE A) and Tree (FIGURE B) intermingle: if the Tree dreams of a well-laid table, the Koala dreams of a roast turkey ready for carving; if the Koala dreams of a ladder made of ice, the Tree dreams of a polar bear in need of ascension.

The key to a successful Pinching Koala and Tree is absolute symbiosis, the kind only found through mutually modulated breathing. Done correctly, the pose leaves its couples feeling like two parts of the same circle, and now that they've found each other, everything rolls smoothly: one person's distaste for doing the dishes is made up for by the other's love of warm, sudsy waters; rat catchers unite with trap makers; and foot fetishists mate with a willing set of perfectly formed toes.

The harmony that comes from this kind of match would be annoying if it weren't so inspirational, which is why Pinching Koalas and Trees are often surrounded by fleets of friends and would-be friends. And on the rare occasion such a couple does dissolve, everyone feels the loss.

PINCHING KOALA AND TREE

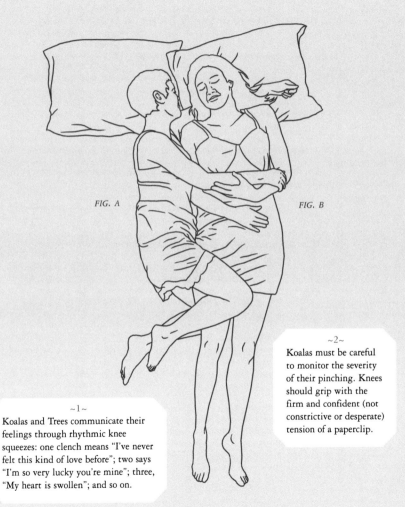

FIG. A   FIG. B

~2~
Koalas must be careful
to monitor the severity
of their pinching. Knees
should grip with the
firm and confident (not
constrictive or desperate)
tension of a paperclip.

~1~
Koalas and Trees communicate their
feelings through rhythmic knee
squeezes: one clench means "I've never
felt this kind of love before"; two says
"I'm so very lucky you're mine"; three,
"My heart is swollen"; and so on.

DOWNWARD KOALA

Koalas dismount a tree by inching down rear-first, paw over paw. But if the temptation is great enough, for instance a tender shoot of mistletoe, the usually cautious koala will make a risky, head-first descent.

Downward Koalas (FIGURE B) can be stirred into similar action, provided they're given the right stimulus. The key is to identify the particular goal that motivates each Downward Koala: does it need to be told that it's smart and lovely? Is it cake it craves? A motorized reclining massage chair? It's up to the Tree (FIGURE A) to figure out what drives its Downward Koala. Because without a reward to look forward to, Downward Koalas can become clingy and spiral into depression, and then their careers stagnate, they gain weight, their creativity wilts, they watch too much television, and they cry and moan. But given something juicy to look forward to, a Koala can go on to lead a full, productive, even happy life.

The Tree, on the other hand, is like the pedestal that elevates a piece of art so that the rest of the world can see its many glorious features: the Tree's happiness comes from nudging/bankrolling the Koala to new heights. As long as the Tree has a Koala to tend to, it doesn't need much else.

DOWNWARD KOALA

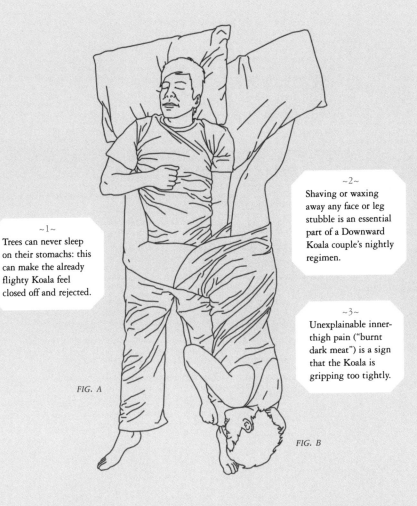

~1~
Trees can never sleep on their stomachs: this can make the already flighty Koala feel closed off and rejected.

FIG. A

~2~
Shaving or waxing away any face or leg stubble is an essential part of a Downward Koala couple's nightly regimen.

~3~
Unexplainable inner-thigh pain ("burnt dark meat") is a sign that the Koala is gripping too tightly.

FIG. B

THE ZIPPER

Couples who sleep as Zippers like to think they're the very first two people on Earth to have stumbled across such a tidily meshed pose. And that's exactly what their parents thought when they first found the position. And their parents' parents before them… all the way back to the bloodstained hammocks of the Vikings. Like penguins returning to their laying grounds, generation after generation, Zipper sleepers always manage to find their way into this pose. And they always find a bedmate with precisely the same inclinations.

Some of it is instinct, but a lot of it is luck, which Zipper sleepers have more than their fair share of. Unexpected promotions always seem to fall into Zippers' laps. Loose chainsaws narrowly miss their heads, and their women come with funnel-shaped uteruses (which make for short, painless labors).

Zipper sleepers also have sharp minds capable of making the kinds of wild connections that can lead to unexpected conclusions: one day they invent some ingenious, million-dollar gadget, the next day they're coloring in a missing eyebrow with a Sharpie.

THE ZIPPER

~1~
Zippers overheat easily.
Make sure to stock towels
and a supply of drinking
water bedside.

~2~
The upper half of the Zipper has
the advantage of a built-in foot
warmer. To avoid a buildup of
resentment, consider alternating
sides night to night.

FIREMAN'S CARRY

True to the heroic connotations of the Fireman's Carry, this is not a position for the gutless. If you're the sort who hesitates before jumping off the high dive or fears intimacy of any kind, then this is not the pose for you.

But never say never: sometimes a readiness for the Fireman's Carry is just a matter of timing. Give yourself a few years. Let yourself fail spectacularly at life and love. For some, the added experience will make you even more wary. But maybe you'll turn out to be the kind of person who finds strength from watching yourself survive setback after setback.

The only way to truly know you're ready for the Fireman's Carry is when you're already doing it. Fireman's Carry couples never decide—they *act*. One minute you're all by yourself, crouched under a pier, lighting matches; the next you're in the very middle of this white-hot embrace, your hearts scorched and scarred and black. But together you're heading for safety.

FIREMAN'S CARRY

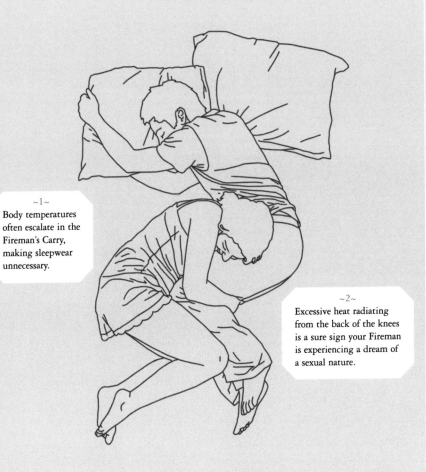

~1~
Body temperatures often escalate in the Fireman's Carry, making sleepwear unnecessary.

~2~
Excessive heat radiating from the back of the knees is a sure sign your Fireman is experiencing a dream of a sexual nature.

SOFTSERVE SWIRL

The 19th-century origins of the Softserve Swirl can be traced to Germany and Austria, where the pose was most likely the product of the Fireman's Carry mixed with the Ventriloquist, and perhaps one or two additional Wind positions. Introduced to the United States in the 1920s, the Softserve Swirl quickly earned the respect of serious sleepers everywhere, who found the position easy to learn and generous in nature.

Couples who spend their nights in the Softserve Swirl position are usually athletic, with backgrounds in many of the netted sports (tennis, volleyball, ping pong). Swirlers also tend to be attractive in the traditional sense. But they're more than just fit bodies and pretty faces: they also have superb criminal instincts. Half of the people on any "Most Wanted" list are Swirlers, as are the majority of police officers. And the couple that inspired the television series *Hart to Hart* (about a married couple of beautiful, independently wealthy detectives, their manservant Max, and his dog Freeway) were both notorious Swirlers.

In short, Softserve Swirlers—with their good looks, felonious minds, and love of volleyball—have what it takes to make crime pay, no matter which side of the law they choose.

SOFTSERVE SWIRL

~1~
Softservers' heads always face toward each other, like sunflowers turning to face their one, true sun.

~2~
A strenuous workout just before bed (cardio and some lifting) can leave the body warmed and limber, the ideal state for Softserve Swirl.

STARFISH AND CONCH

Starfish and Conch is the preferred position of couples who fight well together. If you enjoy the vigor of a good argument—the sparring, the wordplay, the drinks tossed in each other's faces—then the Starfish and Conch position is yours.

Without respite, couples with a taste for battle eventually get tired, causing their warm warring to descend into petty bickering. The only way fighters can stay together for the long haul is if they find a way to reunite in a loving way on a regular basis. The Starfish and Conch position is just that oasis.

The specialties of the Starfish and Conch position are soothing wounds and cooling tempers. After a night of the steady, measured embrace of this pose, couples wake invigorated, the poisonous air between them now cleared of all irritations and misunderstandings. Refreshed and rested, they are ready to take up their shields and swords and go at it again.

Z! 🛏️

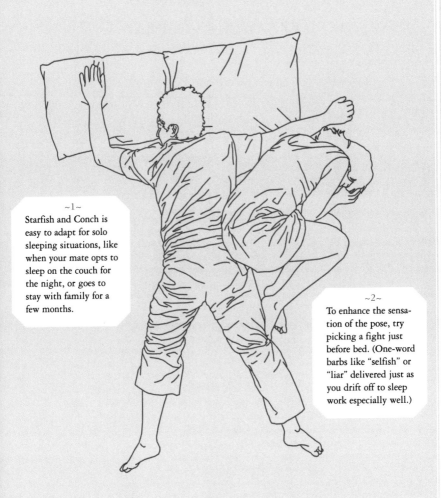

~1~
Starfish and Conch is
easy to adapt for solo
sleeping situations, like
when your mate opts to
sleep on the couch for
the night, or goes to
stay with family for a
few months.

~2~
To enhance the sensa-
tion of the pose, try
picking a fight just
before bed. (One-word
barbs like "selfish" or
"liar" delivered just as
you drift off to sleep
work especially well.)

BREAD AND SPREAD

Every once in a great while two people find each other whose sleeping preferences align so perfectly, the union can't be explained as anything but meant to be. Meet the Bread and Spread.

The Bread and Spread position requires the lucky conjunction of two very special people: someone whose soundest sleep can only be found lying under the significant warmth and weight of another person, and someone who enjoys the precarious position and high-wire balance it takes to spend an entire night lying on top of someone else's shifting body.

Breads (FIGURE B), who, like their namesake, bounce back after being punched down, describe the long nights spent before they found their Spreads (FIGURE A) as "exposed" and "flavorless." And Spreads, who are pliant and accommodating but also tenacious, find any bed partner other than a Bread to be "underchallenging." But once they manage to find each other, few Breads leave their Spreads, and vice versa.

BREAD AND SPREAD

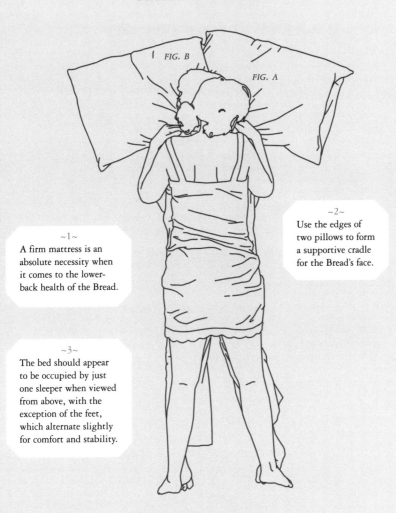

FIG. B

FIG. A

~1~
A firm mattress is an absolute necessity when it comes to the lower-back health of the Bread.

~2~
Use the edges of two pillows to form a supportive cradle for the Bread's face.

~3~
The bed should appear to be occupied by just one sleeper when viewed from above, with the exception of the feet, which alternate slightly for comfort and stability.

THE PATIENT DOCTOR

Named for its resemblance to the twisted snakes and staff of the Caduceus, The Patient Doctor appeals to the rare sort of couple who can live in the same house, commute in the same carpool, work at the same company, and then play in the same band or improv troupe, all without wearing on each other's nerves.

While the very idea of this kind of 9-to-9 proximity panics most couples, Patient Doctors thrive on clock-rounding connectivity, possibly because the whole time they're together, they're all over each other: touching elbows, squeezing ankles, pinching knees, plumping buttocks, cupping chins, patting thighs, hugging with probing hands. Patient Doctors are also famous for they way they coo and purr at each other, and end each other's sentences (which all start with "we").

Coworkers and a smattering of friends endure these off-putting qualities with gritted teeth—much as they weather a shot administered by an actual doctor—and soothe themselves with the thought of how very grateful they are to each of them for taking the other one off the market.

THE PATIENT DOCTOR

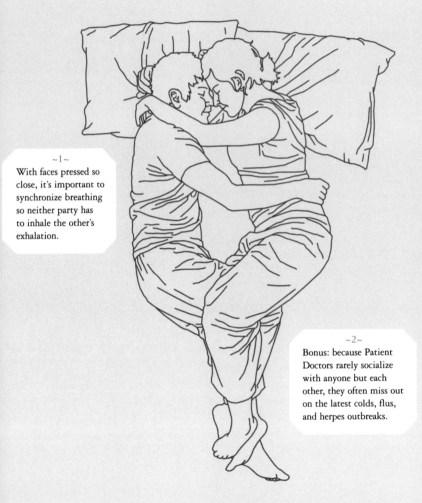

~1~
With faces pressed so close, it's important to synchronize breathing so neither party has to inhale the other's exhalation.

~2~
Bonus: because Patient Doctors rarely socialize with anyone but each other, they often miss out on the latest colds, flus, and herpes outbreaks.

the sea sleepers

The poses of the Sea all focus on symmetry, with added emphasis and meaning coming from the spot where the two reflections meet, which is different for each Sea pose. Venn Trickers' overlapping elbows and knees tell a story of a couple with very, very special needs (skywriting novelists, people who wear wax lips but never kiss, and so on). In The Ticket Puncher pose, a couple's lightly touching toes give voice to the affections of two people with intense personal-space issues. And Sixth Posture of the Perfumed Foresters are so in sync that, even without touching, their bowels rumble on the exact same schedule.

While Sea couples may touch each other in very different ways, they all share a satisfaction with a job well done. Elvis Presley, whose pinky ring and private airplane were emblazoned with the letters T-C-B outlined by the shape of a lightning bolt (i.e., "taking care of business in a flash"), was a notorious Sea sleeper.

SIXTH POSTURE
OF THE PERFUMED FOREST

The stance of the Sixth Posture of the Perfumed Forest is fairly common. Beaches and parks across the world are covered with people relaxing in just this way: on their backs, one hand on stomach, opposite elbow across the eyes. What makes the pose so unusual is its effortless coordination. It may look staged, but Perfumed Forest couples settle into this perfectly reflected position without ever consciously trying to do so.

This kind of accidental perfection indicates a couple that is utterly in sync, no matter how far apart their physical selves travel. Business may take Forester One to France (and then on to Australia) while Forester Two remains at home, tending to livestock. Yet despite the many miles and motivations that separate them, a Sixth Posture of the Perfumed Forest couple always remain tuned to the same rhythm: two photographs, one of each bed, would still splice together seamlessly.

Both sides of a Sixth Posture of the Perfumed Forest couple will report experiencing similar visions as they drift off to sleep. It may be something universal, such as the familiar "falling off the curb" sensation, but their curb will be on the same block, and they'll be wearing the same color shoes, in the middle of the same thunderstorm.

Z! ☀

SIXTH POSTURE OF THE PERFUMED FOREST

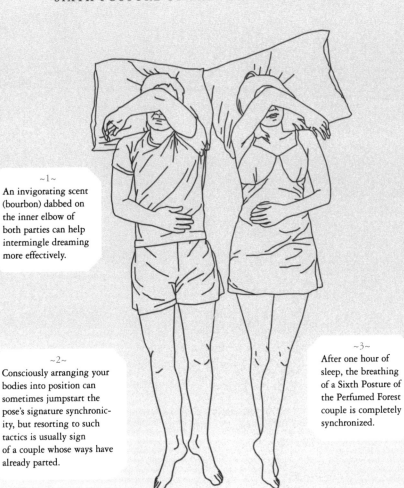

~1~
An invigorating scent (bourbon) dabbed on the inner elbow of both parties can help intermingle dreaming more effectively.

~2~
Consciously arranging your bodies into position can sometimes jumpstart the pose's signature synchronic-ity, but resorting to such tactics is usually sign of a couple whose ways have already parted.

~3~
After one hour of sleep, the breathing of a Sixth Posture of the Perfumed Forest couple is completely synchronized.

PAPER DOLLS

To understand the fundamentals of this position, it helps to actually cut yourself a garland of paper dolls. Fold a piece of paper, accordion style, and then cut out the shape of a human form, being careful to leave the fold intact at the hand and foot. Unfold the paper to reveal the deep sense of attachment that is the very core of Paper Dolls.

Unlike Sixth Posture of the Perfumed Forest couples (see previous), who are capable of enjoying symmetry from afar, Paper Doll couples need to be touching to fall into sync. Stay apart too long, and they start to feel untethered (symptoms: dizziness, unsettled stomach, inability to focus). But a simple brush of the fingers, or a surreptitious foot-on-foot press under the table, is all it takes to reconnect Paper Dolls once more.

Just as a delicate dancer falters without the right partner, Paper Dolls crumple without a perfect match. Ideal Dollmates can be any combination of weight and height, but the pose only works if their feet and hands are the exact same size.

PAPER DOLLS

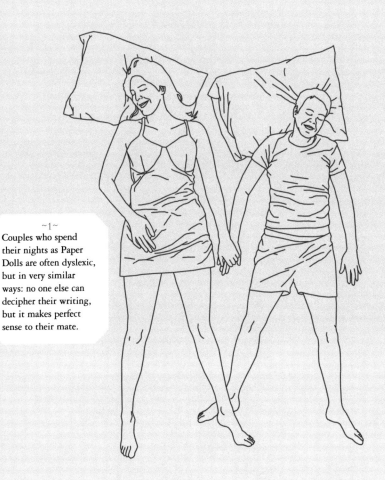

~1~
Couples who spend their nights as Paper Dolls are often dyslexic, but in very similar ways: no one else can decipher their writing, but it makes perfect sense to their mate.

THE BUBBLE BLOWER

As with all Sea positions, the point of connection reveals a great deal about the fundamental nature of the couple. Poses that join at the soles of the feet, as seen here in The Bubble Blower, indicate a couple that is truly equal. The attraction they feel for each other and their level of commitment are both experienced at the exact same level of intensity.

The full circle created by the merged backs and bent legs of this position adds an entirely new dimension to the mix. Circles are signs of transformation, and The Bubble Blower's circle is unusually large, capable of manufacturing huge and wildly different "bubbles." This is the pose of couples in a constant state of life-wide reinvention.

Bubble Blowers enjoy many careers (accountant, painter, driver, consultant, trainer, therapist), and many fads (peanut butter diets, colon cleansers, sticker collections, Europe), and their look is always changing (from mod to soup dragon to robot chic). Yet while they're always doing something new, and it's always vastly different from what the other Bubble Blower is up to, the nightly return to The Bubble Blower pose remains the couple's one reliable constant.

THE BUBBLE BLOWER

~1~
Bubble Blowers always wake at the exact same moment, thanks to subtle flexing in the glutes, which telegraphs each person's gradual ascension to consciousness.

THE CLIFFHANGER

Couples who prefer their eggs not to touch the syrup of their pancakes or who like to keep their needs separated from their wants should already be well familiar with The Cliffhanger.

On the surface, The Cliffhanger might seem like an angry pose, the aftermath of a heated argument or years of misunderstanding. And certainly it's the favorite position of couples that are polar opposites in almost every way: politics, temperament, entertainment tastes, fashion (à la the Schwarzenegger/Kennedy union). Yet even though the bodies of Cliffhanger couples are as far apart as the bed allows, their minds are united regarding the supremacy of personal comfort. Both agree that when it comes to getting a good night's sleep, the sides of the bed are its most prime real estate, and both are practical enough to recognize that the only way for everyone to get the best of the bed is to split up.

This kind of practicality is rare, and while outsiders may puzzle over how and why such publicly different people stay together, Cliffhangers know how precious their one shared trait truly is. As a result, when two Cliffhangers unite, they tend to stick together for the long haul. Except, of course, when it comes to bedtime.

THE CLIFFHANGER

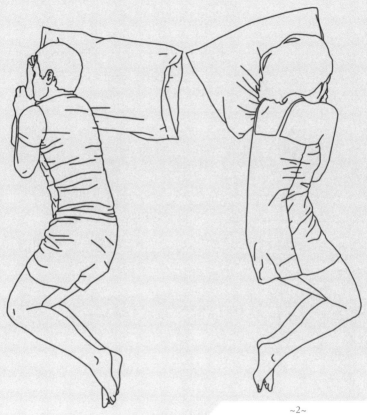

~1~
A foot kicked free of covers regulates a Cliffhanger's temperature and helps to relieve the claustrophobia of monogamy.

~2~
Scarcity of bedding is a common Cliffhanger pitfall. One way to reduce tugging and tension is with separate sets of bedding (two blankets, two sheets, two pillows) or, alternately, one set of double-wide bedding.

VENN TRICK

A Venn diagram (named for its creator, mathematician John Venn, 1834–1923) visually demonstrates the commonalities of two groups using two overlapping circles. For example, some people are fans of '80s boy group New Edition, while some are drawn to the temporary nature of sand sculpture. Still, very, very few people like to spend their weekends at the beach, hand-patting Bell Biv Devoe monuments out of wet sand. In cases like these, the overlap can be so select as to have room for only two people. This is the potential Venn Trick couple.

The Venn Trick pose is defined by the overlapping knees and elbows—the space they contain is the symbolic home for the couple's highly unique preferences and passions. Couples who actually feel comfortable in the position, and can sleep through the discomfort of bony knees and elbows clamped together, are even fewer and farther between than "Candy Girl"-loving sand fans.

VENN TRICK

~1~
The record for the most consecutive hours spent holding the Venn Trick pose: sixty-two.

~2~
The prized Johnny Gill + Sand Castle overlap

THE TICKET PUNCHER

The Ticket Puncher is a favorite position of couples who lead very active, and very separate, lives. They often keep opposite schedules: one will work the night shift, the other the day. One teaches infants to swim every Monday, Wednesday, and Friday, the other paints pregnant belly casts on Tuesdays, Thursdays, and Sundays.

As a result, Ticket Puncher couples can go weeks, even months, without ever seeing each other during waking hours. With so little time to share, the few moments they do manage to come together in sleep are even more precious.

Every aspect of the pose is designed to speak on behalf of a couple that lacks the space, time, and ability for face-to-face communication. The light touch of foot on foot reminds them both that they are missed during the long stretches spent apart, while the great distance between their bodies speaks for how grateful they are to be allowed the freedom their type requires in order for their hearts to grow fonder.

THE TICKET PUNCHER

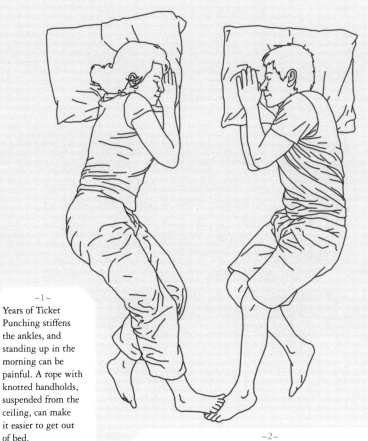

~1~
Years of Ticket Punching stiffens the ankles, and standing up in the morning can be painful. A rope with knotted handholds, suspended from the ceiling, can make it easier to get out of bed.

~2~
With so little free time to express their affection, Punchers let their feet do the hugging and kissing for them, using modulated "gas pedal" pressure to convey a rainbow of feelings.

TOP HAT

The Top Hat pose embodies the light, airy, and effortless movement of Fred Astaire or Elvis Stojko. But as any top-notch performer can tell you, making it look so easy is hard and sweaty work.

The Top Hat is the only pose that features sustained coordinated movement, making it possibly the most demanding of all sleeping positions. Throughout the night, a Top Hat couple will uncross their legs, shift their weight to the opposite foot, windmill their arms, click their heels, and can-can their legs—all in perfect synchronization. Experienced Top Hatters both move as though their arms, hips, feet, and heads are being pulled by the strings of just one puppetmaster.

Unless a Top Hat couple is in prime cardiovascular shape, they will wake each morning exhausted and body-sore, which means that a healthy diet and daily elliptical training are both musts. Team spirit is also essential: pajamas emblazoned with the couple's logo can help put you in the mood.

~1~
A top Top Hat takes practice, practice, and more practice. Couples should plan on spending a minimum of ten hours in bed each night.

THE COLON

As punctuation, the colon is used to alert readers to the presence of things to come, and in many cases the words that follow a colon serve to explain the words that preceded it.

As a sleeping position, The Colon speaks for individuals who could use some explaining. Future Colonists make no sense on their own: they lack spark and context, and they often seem uncomfortable in their own skins. But when a Colonist finds its mate, together they acquire a grace and ease that surprises friends, family, and coworkers.

And their weird little hobbies or physical traits, which made no sense before their Colon formed, suddenly serve a purpose: burp singers fall in with fizzy drink inventors, outies move in with innies, Trekkies meet Renaissance Pleasure Fairies and together their lives become one endless Holodeck, and so on.

Like a string of meaningless words rearranged into a prize-winning story, the two Colonists coalesce, creating a whole that's so very much more than its individual parts.

Z! 🛏

THE COLON

~1~
Colon sleepers are known for their toned diver's bodies, and many male models rely on The Colon to maintain the marketability of their physique.

~2~
A Colonist who is between mates can make do with a tightly curled dog.

the wood sleepers

Wood is the comfort zone of couples who can make something beautiful out of limited resources. Where others see deal-breakers in a bed wetter or drum-and-bugle-corps zealot, Wood sleepers see challenges. And with nimble hands, a good eye, and an impressive ability to adapt (like Springloaders) and compromise (like Tetherballers), Wood sleepers are uniquely equipped to convert challenges into success stories.

But Wooders can play their cards very close to their chests (as evidenced by the behavior patterns of ¡Dormimos!, Scissors, and Conjoined Twins couples), so unless you pay very close attention, ask all the right questions, or have them followed, it can be easy to miss the many things Wood sleepers have to offer.

THE SPRINGLOADER

The unique power of Springloader couples is their ability to find new uses for familiar items. Notice how both Springloaders arrange their legs in a similar way (pressed together and bent), yet each projects a very different kind of energy. While the Spring (FIGURE A) bristles with potential force and energy, and seems to be spoiling for a fight, the Load (FIGURE B) comes off as almost tropically relaxed. Springloaders apply this versatility to every aspect of their lives. They make chairs out of phone books, use hockey sticks as towel hangers, and call tampons cat toys. When they bake pies, they substitute crackers for apples.

This gift for reinvention also allows Springloader couples to wear many hats within the relationship. The Spring goes to work while the Load stays at home and fixes things (the toilet, the attic-wide hornet infestation). The following year, they reverse the roles: Spring takes on domestic duties while Load hunts down the paycheck. The year after that, they embrace an entirely different configuration, sometimes even joining forces with multiple Springloader couples, thereby widening the pool of potential substitutes. (One small warning: when such an alliance forms, it's called a "commune," which can be rife with polyamory, bare feet, and Scandinavians.)

THE SPRINGLOADER

FIG. A

FIG. B

~1~

This position is all about rotation: Springloaders take turns playing Load and Spring, and they lay no claim to a particular side of the bed. And all sleepwear is up for grabs.

¡DORMIMOS! (TRANS: "WE SLEEP!")

Have you ever had a close friend who claims to be in a relationship and yet somehow you never meet this person? For years, your friend shows up at every major event unescorted, always making sure to mention the same steady mate happily waiting at home? This "Snuffleupagus Syndrome" is typical of ¡Dormimos! couples, and it represents a rare and surprisingly winning combination of social butterfly and homebody.

Those of you lucky enough to find yourself in such a pairing may struggle, at first, to find a sleeping position that fits your very different temperaments. Start by spending some time experimenting. After you both have had a turn at left-up, right-down, left-down, and right-up, it's time to sit down and discuss your preferences. If you reach an impasse, consider hiring a specialized "bedroom ombudsperson" to help you negotiate your terms. And if the bickering ever gets truly overwhelming, console yourself with the thought that any couple who masters ¡Dormimos! has the mettle to weather almost any disagreement or sexual dysfunction.

◀)) Z! Ă 🚻 ☀

~1~
¡Dormimos! Inverted

~2~
Every few years try swapping positions for the night. The different perspective can shine new light on an old problem or spice up flagging interests.

TETHERBALL

Couples who come from two different sleeping backgrounds—for example a solitary sleeper and a full-contact sleeper—may at first have trouble finding their perfect symbiotic pose. Conflict, hurt feelings, and guilt can arise when the person who feels suffocated by a bedtime embrace seems to "push away" the one who sleeps best only when held close in a partner's tight grip.

Some might consider such a drastic difference in sleeping preference to be a relationship hurdle. But thanks to the Tetherball position, it doesn't have to be. Tetherball pose allows its Pole (FIGURE B) a free range of movement. Meanwhile Ball's (FIGURE A) tight self-embrace supplies the desired crowded closeness while the supportive gesture of the Pole's arm infuses the position with the necessary spirit of connection.

Note that the Tetherball only works when it's agreed to mutually, after much discussion. Without clear understanding of how the compromise was reached, the generous accommodations the pose represents can be misinterpreted as encroachment. Start the conversation by expressing your original sleeping desire; video footage of a typical night together can sometimes help you articulate your complaints. Only after you both thoroughly understand each other's desires can you begin the slow hunt for the middle ground that is Tetherball.

TETHERBALL

FIG. A

FIG. B

~1~
The Pole's hand is a
scant stand-in for the
full-body embrace
the Ball most craves.
Patting, squeezing,
and buffing motions
can help make up for
the missing comfort
and warmth.

SIDESADDLE

The Sidesaddle is one of the trickier positions, thanks primarily to its mount, which requires a very light touch. First the Pony (FIGURE A) slides into position diagonally across the bed. One to two hours later, when the Pony is deeply asleep and less likely to be skittish, the Rider (FIGURE B) delicately lowers into position. If the Pony stirs at any point, the Rider must be quick with soothing words, a calming caress, a soft lullaby, or some other sleep-inducing trick, because if the Pony wakes fully, it's a complete do-over.

To improve chances of a successful mount, the Pony should come to bed well-primed for sleep—strobing sound-and-light headgear can help, or a job involving heavy manual labor. The Rider should consider actual riding lessons, which will correct any problems with form. But, more than anything, the Rider must know its Pony: which ticklish spots to avoid, which areas respond best to gentle patting, what words are most likely to lure sleep, and which sounds are guaranteed to anger or scare the Pony into instant wakefulness.

On the whole, Sidesaddle sleeping can be a big investment—of time, money, energy—and only select couples (almost always of the "smart-and-controlling + dim-but-pretty" variety) find it worth the cost.

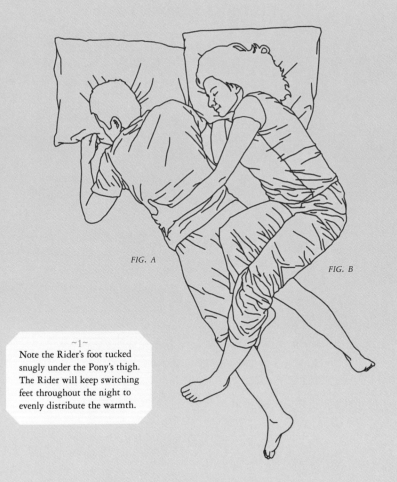

FIG. A

FIG. B

~1~
Note the Rider's foot tucked snugly under the Pony's thigh. The Rider will keep switching feet throughout the night to evenly distribute the warmth.

THE ENCROACHER

To the casual observer, The Encroacher can appear more like combat than an act of mutual rejuvenation. But studied over a series of months, the true nature of the position comes to light. The Encroacher is a position of ebb, flow, give, and take, and couples who are willing to invest in the process truly savor its rewards.

Night one, the eponymous Encroacher takes over the expanse of the bed, leaving the other party to eke comfort in remote corners. In this instance, the Encroacher seems to be getting the better end of the bargain. But check back tomorrow, when Encroacher becomes Encroachee.

The experience of taking turns, of "playing all the parts," gives couples an unusual sense of empathy. Encroachers know how their partners suffer like nobody else. And the rotating experience of scrounging a place to sleep out of limited space is a skill that enhances other aspects of a couple's lives: they wrangle gourmet meals out of leftovers and squeeze impossible amounts of unhangable art into their closets. Encroacher couples need to be careful, however, not to allow themselves to be swept away by their parsimony, which can shrivel into stinginess if not monitored closely.

THE ENCROACHER

~1~

Once the Encroacher has claimed the bulk of the bedspace, the foot and hand no longer shove or repel. Now they gently maintain the connection, steadily communicating affection.

~2~

It's important not to feel guilty when it's your turn as the Encroacher. Rest assured that tomorrow night your bedmate will not hesitate to enjoy the advantage.

STAIRWAY

Structurally speaking, "taking the stairs" is how a person attains a higher plane. In bed, the Stairway achieves a very similar goal: couples describe the way they feel after a night of Stairway as "uplifted" and even "taller."

These elevated aftereffects last well into morning, so couples are advised to schedule any meeting that might benefit from optimism (such as a proposal or motorcycle jump) for the first half of their day. A full week of Stairway can generate a glow that lasts up to an entire month, which is why the position is the number one choice of couples in long-distance relationships.

As little as four weeks of Stairway per year (supplemented by phone calls and written correspondence) is enough to simulate a sense of connection. An entire ocean may divide them, but Stairway-reinforced couples still feel close, possibly because they share the same hyper-realistic dream every night they're apart: that their missing loved one is right there in bed beside them, engaged in full Stairway position.

STAIRWAY

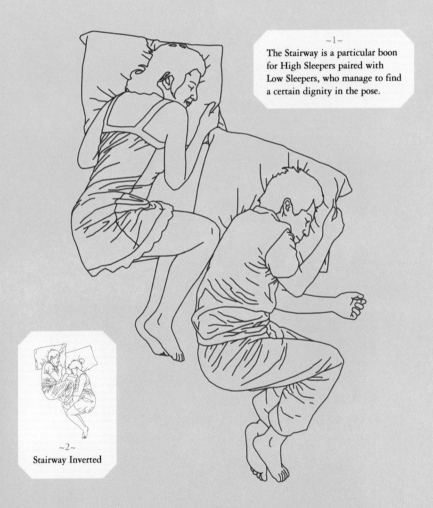

~1~
The Stairway is a particular boon for High Sleepers paired with Low Sleepers, who manage to find a certain dignity in the pose.

~2~
Stairway Inverted

SCISSORS

Scissors is the chosen pose of the kind of couple who nobody realizes is together. They arrive separately at parties and work the room alone all night; only when they leave in the same cab does it occur to anyone that they might actually be taken. This stealthy style can lead to misunderstandings when someone single assumes a solo Scissors is available, but ultimately the approach jibes well with the Scissors couple's independent nature and fierce love of privacy.

Scissors sleepers also have a reputation for making clean breaks with friends, employers, and romantic consorts. At the time, their abrupt adieus can be startling. But their no-fuss splits tend to heal more cleanly, and scar over more quickly, than other people's agonized and over-discussed breakups. This makes it far easier for friendships to re-form years down the line, which is why Scissors couples are in such good standing with so many of their exes—so much so that they frequently have multiple exes over to dinner simultaneously.

In most cases, the Scissors way of life is instinctive. But with conscious effort, and many nights spent acclimatizing to the constant leg movement and stomach-down technique, some people do manage to adopt the tidy goodbyes and secretive ways of born Scissors.

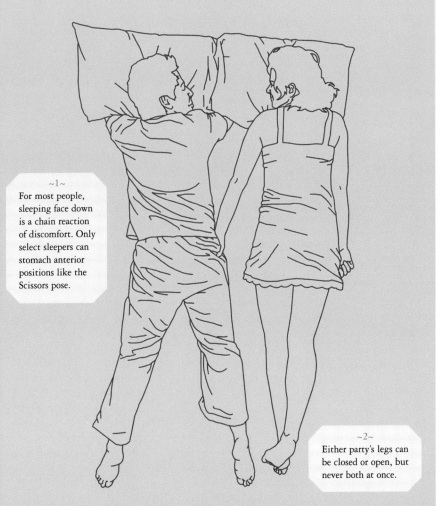

~1~
For most people, sleeping face down is a chain reaction of discomfort. Only select sleepers can stomach anterior positions like the Scissors pose.

~2~
Either party's legs can be closed or open, but never both at once.

PILLOW TALK, PILLOW LISTEN

The sounds of your bedmate's most fundamental inner workings reveal a great deal about what's most troubling or pleasing him or her. Spending an evening listening to what's percolating can help you gauge the successes and challenges that loom before you both. High-pitched, dolphin-style squeaks can mean your partner is preparing to take things to the next level. Geiger-counter clicks indicate potential money troubles. Groans or meows are signs of too much dairy.

Couples who engage in Pillow Talk, Pillow Listen must pay close attention to the comfort of their bedmates. Underweight Pillows (FIGURE A) can make an uncomfortable resting spot for Listeners (FIGURE B), so they should switch to a "fry and pie" diet until the necessary layer of soft fat forms. Similarly, Listeners have to remove earrings or headgear before bed to protect their partner's underbelly from unwanted scratches or piercings.

PILLOW TALK, PILLOW LISTEN

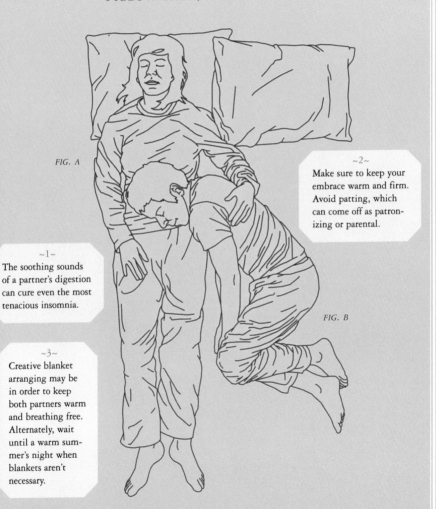

FIG. A

FIG. B

~1~
The soothing sounds of a partner's digestion can cure even the most tenacious insomnia.

~2~
Make sure to keep your embrace warm and firm. Avoid patting, which can come off as patronizing or parental.

~3~
Creative blanket arranging may be in order to keep both partners warm and breathing free. Alternately, wait until a warm summer's night when blankets aren't necessary.

TURNSTILE

The Turnstile is the position of transition and demarcation. Couples who find themselves sleeping in this pose should listen closely, because big changes are warming up on deck.

In some cases, the Turnstile indicates a couple that is gearing up to take things to the next level, whether it's marriage, cohabitation, or a shared pet rescued from the woods behind the shed. But most of the time, the Turnstile represents dark, dark clouds gathering on the horizon.

You may not have admitted this to each other yet, or even to yourselves, but one or both of you is significantly dissatisfied with the way things are going. It's possible that you're struggling with attractions outside the relationship, or maybe it's a simple matter of boredom or chronic irritation. But whatever your problem may be, if it's reached the Turnstile level, it's probably significant.

So take a long, hard look, Turnstilers. Is it time to move on? Or time to pop the question? Your mattress knows.

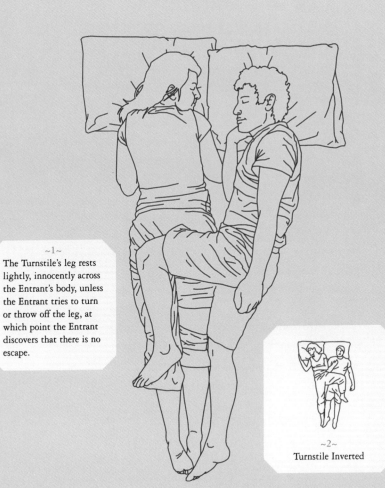

~1~
The Turnstile's leg rests lightly, innocently across the Entrant's body, unless the Entrant tries to turn or throw off the leg, at which point the Entrant discovers that there is no escape.

~2~
Turnstile Inverted

CONJOINED TWINS, HEAD (CRANIOPAGUS)

Couples who sleep joined at the head are intelligent, busy thinkers with shy, quiet ways. The one exception to their tight-lipped nature is their bedmates, to whom they open up without any reserve. Because Conjoined Twin couples so obviously prefer each other's company above all else, they are sometimes thought of as exclusive or even stuck up. And, strictly speaking, this is true: anyone outside the Conjoined Twin couple will always be second rate.

Fortunately not many Twins are concerned with how they're perceived by the outside world. But in the rare cases that other people's opinions matter (perhaps in a business situation or when running for office), Twins can sometimes overcompensate in their attempts to simulate real affection, and will shower outsiders with wildly inappropriate gifts (cars, underwear emblazoned with uncomfortable slogans) or stand far too close. Before long, coworkers and constituents learn to steer clear, which, happily, lets Twins return to their naturally antisocial behaviors.

CONJOINED TWINS, HEAD (CRANIOPAGUS)

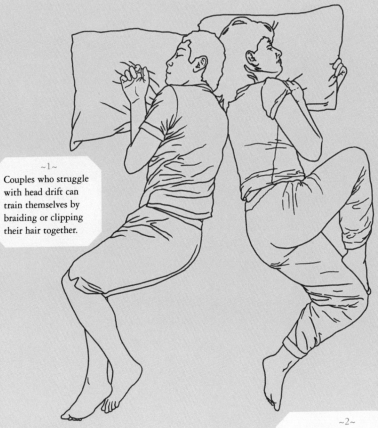

~1~
Couples who struggle with head drift can train themselves by braiding or clipping their hair together.

~2~
Conjoined Twins pose is sometimes the temporary choice of couples chastened by a visit to a parents' home.

CRIME SCENE

Despite the brutality of its name, the Crime Scene position is anything but violent. Crime Scene sleepers are actually very sensitive, creative, and inoffensive creatures, and aside from their dreams— which are blood-splattered horrors full of spine-splitting screams and drilling sounds—Crime Scenesters have no significantly disturbing tendencies.

Couples who find themselves drawn to the Crime Scene position tend to be individualists who thrive in loosely structured environments with few or no confining dress codes, and they often make fine phlebotomists.

This relaxed approach to life is reflected in the pose itself: unlike the Stairway or Sidesaddle poses, the Crime Scene is entirely freeform. Scenesters sprawl into whatever position holds the most personal comfort or meaning. The only constant of the pose is that the couple must touch in some small way: a finger brushing neck or knee touching flank is enough to keep the Crime Scene intact.

Z! 🛏 ☀

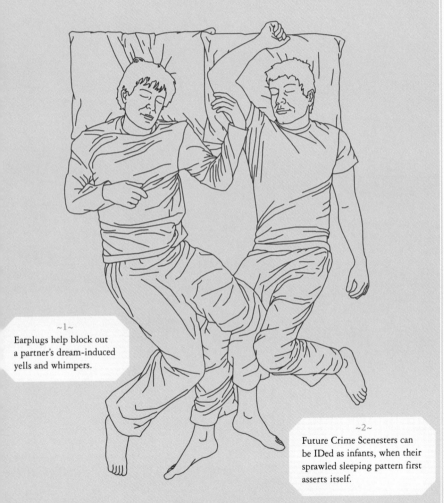

~1~
Earplugs help block out
a partner's dream-induced
yells and whimpers.

~2~
Future Crime Scenesters can
be IDed as infants, when their
sprawled sleeping pattern first
asserts itself.